Creating Custom Art Tiles

Stamps and Stencils

Jaye Slade Fletcher

JolieFaire Tile

Copyright Jaye Slade Fletcher 2008

ISBN # 1440498520

TABLE OF CONTENTS

GETTING STARTED: THE BASICS　　　　PAGES 1-12

Plaster Molds　　　　PAGES 13-19

PART ONE: STAMPS　　　　PAGES 20-44

What are we talking about?　　　　PAGES 20-26

Stamps and Clay　　　　PAGES 27-31

Let's Make a Tile!　　　　PAGES 32-39

Variations and After-Thoughts　　　　PAGES 40-44

PART TWO: STENCILS　　　　PAGES 45-80

What are we talking about?　　　　PAGES 46-53

Stencils and Clay　　　　PAGES 54-59

Let's Make a Tile!　　　　PAGES 60-73

Variations and After-Thoughts　　　　PAGES 74-79

Conclusion　　　　PAGE 80

GETTING STARTED: THE BASICS
MATERIALS LIST

Raw ceramic clay

Ceramic slip

Plaster of Paris

Corn starch

Small foam brushes and clay-working tools

Small spray bottle

Small square of 1/2" or 3/4" sheetrock

Craft knives

Stamps and Stencils

In this book, we are going to learn, step by step, how to design and carve custom relief tiles using two very different methods—first, we'll discuss Stamps and then in Part Two, we'll discuss Stencils.

Whatever method we use to create and build a new custom-designed art tile, we need to be sure we have the basics down pat. Just as though we were building a house, we want to be sure our foundation is true and solid before we start building complicated stuff on top of it. It's nearly impossible to go back and fix a faulty 'foundation' once you've built on top of it—far better to use sufficient thought and care to get it right the first time.

As a general rule, your Base Tile should be a minimum 1/4" thick if you're making a 4" tile—a minimum of 3/8" thick if you're making a 6" tile, and so on upward. Any thinner than that and you risk your tile curling or warping during firing. You can, of course, make your Base Tile much thicker if you're looking for that special effect. I have produced many 'special effect' tiles as thick as one and a half inches. Any thicker than that, and you might have problems getting the tile to dry properly. The outside of the tile might become bone dry, but there could still be moisture trapped deep in the center of the tile, and then the piece would explode in the kiln. Because tile-making is my business, I have a range of professional tools and equipment on hand, such as a slab roller and various tile-cutters. For the casual hobbyist though, such expensive equipment isn't really necessary.

A rolling pin can be used to roll out a good smooth Base Tile.

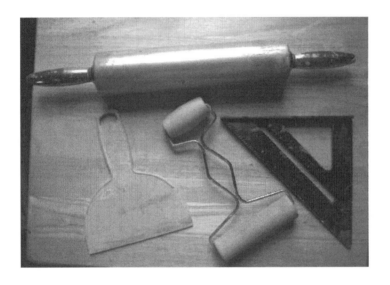

An ordinary plastic trowel is great for smoothing the surface of the tile. And various tools can be used to cut the tile to shape. The common needle tool is often used to cut clay shapes, including tiles. But this is my least favorite cutter. Because the needle is round, it leaves an unpleasant raised ridge along either side of the cut line. It also causes the clay to distort and get dragged out of shape as you're pulling it through the clay.

My favorite method of manually cutting tiles is the pizza cutter, available in the kitchen utensils section of your grocery or department store.

I've used these same two pizza cutters for many years. The smaller one was less than $2. It has a very thin metal blade which is useful for finely-detailed trimming and shaving, but it's not at all good for cutting out thick heavy tiles. The little blade is wobbly (can't imagine cutting a pizza with this!) The larger pizza cutter is one of my favorite all-time clay-working tools. Big solid blade, comfortable handle with finger grips, and it costs less than $10.

TIP: When choosing a pizza cutter for your clay work, look for one with a large sturdy blade that is beveled. The beveled edge gives you a clean, crisp cut.

TIP: When using your pizza cutter to cut out a tile, angle your blade ever so slightly inward toward the top of the tile as you're cutting, to avoid undercuts.

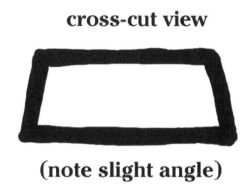

cross-cut view

(note slight angle)

Hold your cutter blade at a very slight angle, so that your tile is slightly wider at the bottom .

If you're going to invest in tile cutters, there are some things to watch out for. Tile cutters are expensive and you want to look for the ones that will give you the best performance. The two square tile cutters in this photo are excellent. The hexagon cutter is not.

The square cutters measure 4 1/4" and 6 ½" respectively. Allowing for shrinkage during drying and firing, these square cutters will produce 4" or 6" tiles. They are made of razor-thin copper walls with a hard maple roof. The inside floor of the cutter is lined with hard foam padding, which produces a clean, smooth surface on your tile. They cost about $40 ea at most large clay-supply outlets.

The hexagon cutter is made of quite thick steel walls and it doesn't produce the same crisp, clean cut as does the razor-thin copper. Also, when I bought this hexagon cutter ($60 !!) the inside floor (which presses down against your clay) was bare metal, with a rivet in the center. Ridiculous! Every tile you cut with this would have the same imprint of a rivet right in the middle of your tile. I went out and bought some thick green felt, cut it to size, peeled off the backing and glued it to the cutter floor. This has helped somewhat, although any tile I cut with this cutter still shows a slight indentation from the rivet. Grrrr....

If you're in the market for a tile cutter, I'd suggest a visit to your local ceramics supply warehouse. That way, you can actually see and hold the cutter, in person. I don't live anywhere near such a supply center, so I have to buy my supplies on line. Usually, that works out pretty well, but I have to admit, every time I look at this $60 hexagon cutter, well…

Grrrrr….

PLASTER MOLDS

When you've finished making your prototype relief tile, whether you use Stamps or Stencils, you'll probably want to make a mold from it so you can reproduce endless 'clone' tiles from that same original design. While this book is not a tutorial about making plaster molds, here's a brief overview.

Commercially available plaster comes in three grades. The cheapest is chalk, which is what most commercial tile molds are made of–I don't like using cheap chalk for my molds, since it's extremely brittle and fragile. The next grade is Plaster of Paris, and the most-expensive grade is hydro-cal. Hydro-cal isn't useful for our purposes since it is so extremely dense and hard that it doesn't absorb the moisture out of your slip-poured tiles. It is meant to be used in molds designed for heavy-duty tile-press machines.

Plaster of Paris is inexpensive and readily available at Wal-Mart, craft shops and home centers like Lowe's or Home Depot. It comes in 5 lb plastic buckets or in large 25-lb and 50-lb bags.

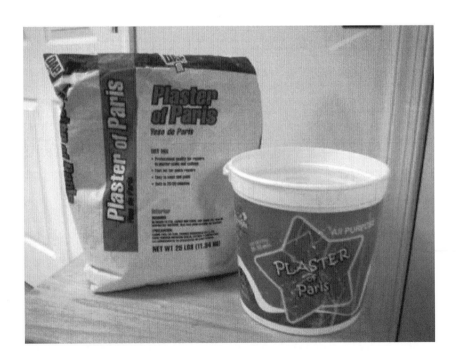

I paid about $6 for this bucket of plaster and only about $9 for the 25-lb bag of plaster. Obviously, the 25-lb bag is the better bargain, though it might be more than you need if you're only thinking of making one or two molds.

I use ordinary plastic food-storage containers to make my molds. (Never use glass, wood or metal–the plaster will adhere to the container and you'll never get it out.)

The smaller containers in this photo will require about 2 large (16 oz) cups of water, the larger container about 3 ½ large cups.

Using a plastic bucket, mix your plaster with cold water at a 2:1 ratio. That is, 2 cups of plaster to 1 cup of COLD water.

ALWAYS add the plaster to the water, never the other way around. Sprinkle the plaster into the water little at a time while stirring slowly with a paint stir stick or something similar. Slow stirring helps keep down the air bubbles which will form in the plaster mix.

Lift the bucket several inches off the floor and drop it, heavily. Doing this 8 or 10 times will force any trapped air bubbles to the surface, where yo can break them with your stir stick. Set your raw tile in the container and pour several inches of plaster over it.

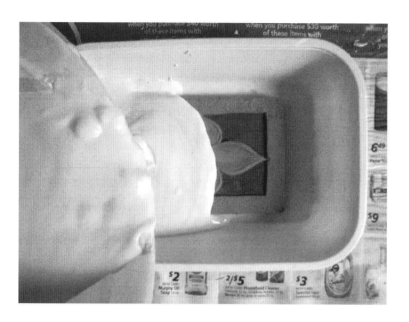

Jiggle the container back and forth slightly to even out the surface of your plaster. Allow the new mold to 'cure' for at least several hours before prying out your tile. You'll notice some interesting chemical changes going on while your plaster is curing. It will become quite hot, and will then turn very cold and form a film of 'sweat' on the surface.

Pry your tile out of the mold carefully. The plaster is still quite soft at this stage and will scratch very easily.

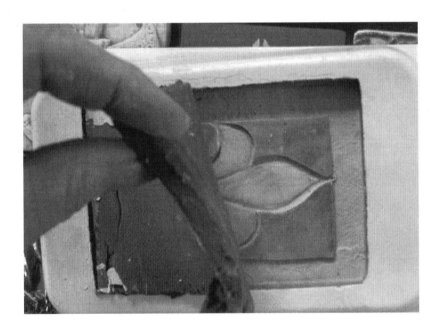

Your original prototype tile will be ruined by this molding process, in that it will have bits of plaster stuck to it. But, not to worry! You now have a mold from which you can make an unlimited number of identical tiles. Use your loop tool to clean and square the edges of your new mold.

PART ONE

STAMPS

WHAT ARE WE TALKING ABOUT?

When I use the word 'stamps,' I'm talking about the red rubber raised-relief art stamps available in craft stores, on-line sites, and on eBay. Here are some of my own stamps.

You purchase such stamps either 'mounted,' or 'unmounted. 'Unmounted' means that you're purchasing only the rubber stamp itself, with no sort of backing. 'Mounted' means you're purchasing the stamp which is glued to some sort of backing, usually a maple wooden block.

The photo on the back of the block mount will be positioned exactly as the rubber stamp is positioned on the other side, which allows you to know exactly where on your page (or your tile) the image will appear. Mounted stamps are many times more expensive than unmounted stamps, since you're also buying the maple block and photo.

<u>TIP:</u> Maple is a very hard, dense wood and is excellent for all sorts of clay-working tools, since it doesn't absorb moisture and swell as do softer woods such as pine or spruce.

Rubber art stamps are also available as rollers, which offer many different and interesting designs. The roller-wheel stamps pictured here are by a company called *Stampin' Up*.

The individual roller-wheels are inter-changeable and snap easily into and out of the handle.

Here's an example of a roller-wheel checkerboard pattern being rolled into clay. (I brushed the roller-wheel with a little black underglaze so the pattern would show up more clearly in this photo.)

Here are some makers of rubber art stamps, but there are many more out there, as you'll see when you Google 'rubber stamp'!

Stamps Happen   *Addicted to Rubber Stamps*

Mother Rubber Art Stamps   *PSX Stamps*

Stampin' Up   *The Stampin' Place*

Hero Arts OnLine   *Magenta*

To find such stamps on eBay, go to ebay.com. Enter 'rubber stamp' in the search bar, or refine your search according to your interest, such as 'rubber stamp celtic,' 'rubber stamp roller' etc.

Many objects other than rubber stamps can be used to stamp impressions into clay, of course. This photo shows a few wooden block stamps. These are actually fabric stamps from India, but their open, clear designs makes them ideal for pressing into clay.

Wooden stamps like these were used during the Middle Ages to create those wonderful Medieval tiles that still adorn many of Europe's great cathedrals. You can also, of course, use fancy buttons, appliques, etc. to add interest to your tile.

-

STAMPS AND CLAY

I have wasted a great deal of money over the years buying rubber art stamps that proved to be useless for working with clay. The primary purpose for all of these stamps is, of course, for stamping designs on paper, using colored ink.

For paper and ink, it's okay to use a stamp that has microscopically tiny and shallow design elements. For clay, though, such stamps just don't work. Look at this stamp.

You can see that the design consists of wide, rounded cuts. This is an excellent stamp for impressing into clay.

Now, look at this stamp of a Medieval gryphon, with its very narrow cuts in the tail, wings and front claws, and the tiny, shallow design in the head and body area.

The shallow body design won't make a clear impression in clay. Even worse, the deep, very narrow cuts in the tail, wings and claws trap your clay and when you lift the stamp off of the clay, those bits will tear off of your tile and remain embedded in the stamp.

I've wasted even more money over the years buying mounted stamps (like this charming tree frog), only to realize once I began to work with them that I have much more control and precision in creating my tile using unmounted stamps.

I ended up ripping the rubber stamps off of all the mounting blocks, and I now have a box full of expensive maple blocks that I didn't need to buy! The only time I would now buy a mounted stamp would be if I fell in love with a particular design and simply could not find it unmounted.

TIP: If you do have a few of those unneeded maple mounting blocks around, don't throw them away! They can be used as handy tools, as described in one of my other books 'Creating Custom Art Tiles: Slips and Presses.'

The only rubber stamps that I do leave mounted on their wooden blocks are the very tiny ones, which I call 'dot stamps' or 'element stamps.' The little star stamps you see here, for example, are just 1/4" and would be nearly impossible to work with if they were not mounted.

LETS MAKE A TILE!

For this demonstration, we're going to use the Celtic square rubber stamp (p. 27) to make a tile—you may wish to build a more complicated and detailed tile design using your own stamps, of course, but for this book I want to take large, clear, easy-to-see photos such as I'll get using this stamp.

The sequence of steps we'll use to create our new prototype tile will depend on whether we're using (1) a pizza cutter, or (2) a tile cutter. Using the pizza cutter method will distort the shape of your Base Tile; using the tile cutter will not. (I'll explain as we go along.)

Method #1

This particular Celtic square stamp measures 2 ½" so I'm going to make a 4" tile. You can use it to make any size tile you like, of course. I want my new finished tile to be about 1/4" thick, so I've rolled out my clay somewhat thicker than that, since pressing the stamp into the clay will compress the thickness of the clay. Brushing the surface of your clay with corn starch will help assure a nice, clean impression, as it keeps the clay and stamp from sticking together.

Next, lay your rubber stamp, design side down, on the clay. Use a rolling pin to press the stamp evenly into the clay, rolling lightly back and forth until the back of the stamp is even with the surface of the clay. Pressing with a rolling pin like this will distort the shape of your clay slab, which is why we didn't cut our tile to a 4" square beforehand. Use the tip of your needle tool to lift the stamp up off the clay.

Smooth away any little needle-tool nicks or scratches with the tip of your dampened finger.

The stamp has made a nice, clear impression in the clay. Now, we can size the tile and cut it with the pizza cutter.

Use the edge of a plastic trowel, or any similar thin straight-edge to lightly mark the outlines of the tile.

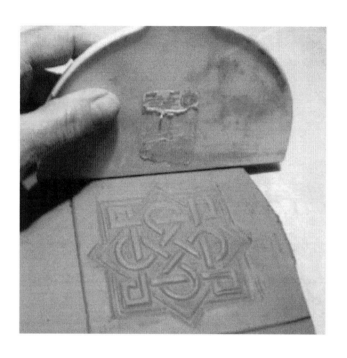

If you find it difficult to create a perfect square using free-hand methods like this, you can use a small, lightweight t-square to be sure your tile shape is perfectly squared. Then, use your large pizza cutter to cut your tile.

Method # 2

Here, we're going to start out the same way, pressing the stamp, design-side down, into the clay slab. But then, we'll use a copper 4" tile cutter to cut the tile.

Laying the tile cutter over the clay and stamp, I tapped all around the edges of the cutter with a rubber mallet. Lifting the tile cutter, I've now got a perfectly square new tile. Because the clay wa contained within the four walls of the tile cutter, it did not distort out of shape while being pressed.

Mixing up some plaster of Paris, I'll make a mold of my new prototype tile.

As you'll note in this photo, you've reached the right ratio of plaster to water when your sprinkled plaster begins to sit, dry, on the surface of your mixture. This means that every molecule of water in your bucket has absorbed a molecule of plaster, and no more can be absorbed.

I poured the plaster mix into my plastic mold container. I then allowed the plaster mold to cure for several hours before prying the clay tile out of it. Any minor little flaws can easily be shaved smooth using a small loop tool. The plaster is very soft at this stage and is easy to carve.

Unless you plan on going into business, you probably won't end up with as many tile molds as I have. Still, it's a good idea to write the name of the tile on the edge of the mold, using an indelible marker. Once they're all stacked up like this, it would be impossible to tell which design is in which mold, without this 'label.'

VARIATIONS AND AFTER-THOUGHTS

When you press a stamp into clay, the relief design on the stamp will be reversed on the clay. For example, look at the wings on this beautiful butterfly-lady stamp (right). Then, look at the impressed clay (left).

You can see that the wing partitions which were in raised relief on the stamp are now impressed into the clay. With some stamps, that wouldn't matter much (our Celtic square, for example.)

But, for this stamp, that's not a particularly pleasant reversal.

If you were to make a plaster mold of the clay piece on the left, the wing partitions in the mold design would be in raised relief again. Great, right? Not! Because then, every tile you made from that mold would again have the relief designs reversed.

Here's how we'll fix that problem, using the butterfly-lady stamp as our example. We're going to press the butterfly lady stamp into a piece of soft polymer clay. (I prefer Sculpey, but there are other brand-name polymer clays out there.) Lay out a piece of your Sculpey and roll it out flat and smooth.

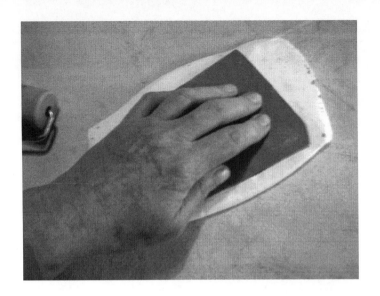

Then, press the butterfly stamp into it. I use my fingertips rather than the rolling pin for this step because polymer clay is much more plastic, much less easily 'impressible' than is ceramic clay. You have to use some pressure to get a good clear impression.

Bake your polymer clay per the box directions— with Sculpey, its about 15 or 20 minutes in the kitchen oven. Let the Sculpey cool, then press a smooth piece of ceramic clay onto it, using your rolling pin. Be a bit gentle with this part, since polymer clay, once baked, is quite brittle and breaks easily.

As you see, we now have a raised relief butterfly-lady again!

(I could have pressed my ceramic clay a bit harder into the polymer—you can see around the feet that I didn't get a perfect impression. If this happens to you, just knead your ceramic clay, roll it out again and take another, clearer impression.)

Now, if we were to make a plaster mold of the ceramic clay butterfly-lady, the design inside the plaster mold would be reversed, but then every tile we made from that mold would again show the raised relief design, just like the original stamp!

PART II

STENCILS

WHAT ARE WE TALKING ABOUT?

When I use the word 'stencil' in this book, for the most part I'm talking about the white mylar stencils widely available on crafts shops and via many on-line sites. Since making art tiles is my business, I have many hundreds of stencils. A few, like the little grapes-and-leaves stencil in the lower right of this photo,

I have purchased at Wal-Mart or other stores.

But my tile specialty is Medieval design, so I have searched far and wide for my stencils, and have even had quite a few of them custom made. 'Stencil' for this book's purposes can also mean brass stencils, also available (cheap!) in crafts shops and on-line sites.

You can make your own stencils, too, using blank sheets of mylar and a sharp craft knife to cut out your own designs. I've never had any success with this, though. I simply cannot achieve the perfect precision that machine-cut stencils offer.

Of the many on-line stencil sites, I have two top favorites, each of them being a favorite for different reasons. Please understand that I have no financial interest in either of these companies—I simply pass along this info after having dealt very happily with both sites for years. The first favorite is Stencil Planet. (www.stencilplanet.com) They're one of my favorites because they offer, not only a wide range of interesting stencils, but also custom stencil-making services. I've had them custom make many stencils from designs I supplied them, and I've always been pleased with their work. Custom-made stencils can be expensive (in the $100 range, up or down depending on size and complexity). And, you must supply them with a clear, camera-ready image from which to work. There are millions of copyright-free images available on the web, just do a Google Image

Search for your favorite designs, and you'll see what I mean.

Besides doing web searches, I've also found some of my custom designs in books. From a copyright-free children's coloring book of guardian angels, I found a design which I call 'Stained Glass Angel.' I took a digital photo of that page, sent the photo to Stencil Planet with an inquiry as to price, and then had them make the stencil for me. (Email them at info@stencilplanet.com) When they cut a custom stencil for you, they will email you for your approval before actually cutting it, which is great. A couple of times, I asked for slight alterations, which they readily did. Stencil Planet was so fond of some of my designs that they asked for (and got) my permission to include my designs in the stencil catalog. The 'Stained Glass Angel' is among the designs they now offer. If you look at the cover of this book, you can see an example of the Stained Glass Angel tile I made from this stencil.

Another of my designs now included in the Stencil Planet catalog is a set of three Medieval playing cards.

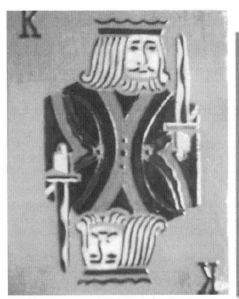 

I found these designs in a copyright-free illustrated book of playing cards. (I mention these various sources just to indicate how wide a range you have in choosing your own custom stencil design.) You can see a finished tile made from this stencil on the cover of this book.

My other favorite on-line stencil store is The Stencil Library. (www.stencil-library.com) They're on my favorites list because they simply have more, and more unique, and more unusual stencils than anyplace else I've seen. Beware, though, my fellow American tile artists. The Stencil Library is in England, and with the American dollar currently worth ½ a British pound, these stencils are expensive! One very clever idea among many at The Stencil Library is movie star stencils—line drawings of such famous, fabulous faces as Humphrey Bogart, Audrey Hepburn, Claudette Colbert, etc.

I didn't buy their movie star stencils, but being fairly adept at free-hand drawing myself, I looked around on the web for suitable images and started painting movie star tiles myself. Here's my Barbara Stanwyck and Janet Leigh. Great fun

TIP: An excellent place to look for custom stencil ideas is at your local wallpaper shop. Wallpaper

designs are precision machine cut and available in thousands of patterns, everything from flowers to children's designs to jungle creatures. And, you can usually get a small wallpaper sample for free or for very little money. You can then trace the wallpaper design onto a sheet of mylar and cut out your own custom stencil.

STENCILS AND CLAY

Remember, in the Stamps section of this book, we looked at and discussed certain stamp designs that simply aren't suitable for working in clay? The same applies to stencils. This stencil is excellent for clay work.

The incised lines are wide and open. Just as when you're working with stamps, you don't want teensy little incised cuts in your stencil. Your clay will simply get trapped in those crevices and will tear apart when you try to lift the stencil off of the clay. (Look at the cover of this book to see how pretty this tile looks in color, finished and glazed.) You can see that in designing this tile, I added some raised design that's not on the stencil. I simply used another stencil to add that design, a Medieval border design from the Stencil Library.

In talking about stencils that won't work for clay, I'll relate here a very serious mistake that I made—one that has caused me no end of distress and annoyance. I had Stencil Planet custom make these three wonderful stencils for me. They are The Gates of Moria, The White Tree of Gondor and The Rohan Horse Banner, all from the Lord of the Rings movies.

I am an LOTR fan and I knew that tiles made from these images would be wildly popular–which they are. I had to search long and hard to find clear, camera ready images. Remember, you can't send a vague, angled photo and ask the stencil-maker to 'straighten it out.' They can only use the exact photo you send them. At last, I found my three clear images. I then worked with them in my Adobe Photoshop, erasing various extraneous bits. I sent the images to Stencil Planet and had them make the stencils for me.

BUT! I have had nothing but trouble and aggravation from day one working with these expensive stencils—and it's all my own fault! Look at how tiny and narrow those little hair-like roots of the tree are—and how tiny and narrow are the inter-twined circles up in the body of the tree. My LOTR tiles are very popular, but every single new tile I make from these stencils has to be carefully and tediously fixed and patched by hand before I can fire it. Every time I lift these stencils off of a new tile, the clay tears or sticks in those tiny crevices. I then have to use matching slip and a very small artist's brush (I call it my 'three-hair brush') to dab in and fix the roots and circles by hand. The Gates of Moria stencil is just as bad. All those teensy little symbols in the arch are elvish writing, and the three incised lines at the bottom of the pillars are also way too narrow for clay—the clay tears at those points, every single time.

This was my mistake—not Stencil Planet's. I should have asked them (now I know!) to make all incised lines at least 1/8" wide, like they are o[n] the Rohan Banner.

Another mistake I made when having these stencils cut—because I didn't know any better at the time—was that I didn't ask for them to be cut from heavier mylar. The average thickness for a mylar stencil is .005 millimeters. But, you can ask for them to be cut using .010 mil mylar, or even .014 mil. Clay and slip are thick, heavy materials to work with, and the thin .005 mil mylar, when cut into teensy little lines, is simply too fragile. I now have tears in both my Moria and White Tree stencils, because some of those tiny little lines simply broke when I lifted the stencil off the clay.

Learn from my mistakes!

-

-

-

LETS MAKE A TILE!

For this book demonstration, I'm going to make two tiles, each using slightly different variations. I'll use two of my favorite stencils from The Stencil Library–my Knight Templar (that's what I call it–the Stencil Library simply calls this stencil 'Knight No. 2 and their Fleur de-lis Tile No. 1.

For my Knight Templar, I'll use a dark clay body (terra cotta) with a white slip design. For the

Fleur-de-lis, I'll use a light buff clay body with a chocolate brown underglaze design.

Using slip to create your design will give you a raised relief design. Using underglaze instead of slip will give you only color, not raised relief. So, if you intend to make a plaster mold of your tile in order to reproduce more tiles from the same design, then you'll want to use slip, not underglaze, to create your design.

<u>TIP:</u> There's no need to buy expensive colored slips. You will actually use very little slip to make your raised relief tile design, so just put a few tablespoons of slip into a small bowl and add a tablespoon of underglaze to color it. Stir well, and there's your colored slip!

I rarely make plaster molds of my stencil-designed tiles, unless I know I will be glazing those tiles in a single color. Otherwise, I would have to paint in the design by hand on each tile. To me, it seems easier (and less tedious!) to cut each new two-color tile individually. Take this Celtic Cross tile, for example.

I made this design from a brass stencil, and I made a plaster mold from the prototype tile. I glazed the white bisque tile with a sapphire blue gloss glaze, wiping the dried glaze away from the raised design so the cross would show up better. But, what if I'd wanted to make the raised cross design a completely different color? I would have to hand-paint the cross with underglaze. Too much work! Instead, I simply use my brass stencil to make a new, two-color tile each time I want one.

TIP: Brass stencils, unlike mylar stencils, will give you a raised relief design 'automatically,' without the addition of slip. The clay of the base tile will squish up (that's the scientific term—squish up...) into the cut-outs in the brass.

This photo shows you the nice, crisp raised relief

design you get from pressing a brass stencil into raw moist clay.

I use a slab roller, so I've rolled out my white and my terra cotta slabs at the same time.

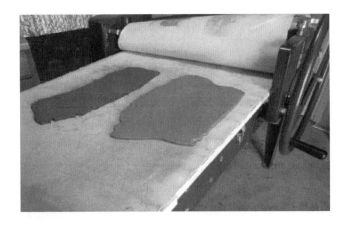

Brush the surface of your clay with corn starch.

This is an important step—the mylar is going to want to stick to your clay, and if it does, you'll end up with a pocky, pebbled surface on the tile once you lift the stencil up. (Corn starch, being simply a vegetable-based powder, will burn off harmlessly during firing, and won't alter or damage your tile at all.)

Use your rolling pin to flatten the stencil into the surface of the clay. It's important that you get a good adhesion onto the clay surface, because if you don't, then your slip or underglaze will seep under the stencil and ruin your design. You can see in this photo what I mean. Look at the upper left of the stencil, just at the knight's shoulder.

See that white spot between the shoulder and the edge of the stencil? That's air, trapped between the stencil and the clay. If I were to brush slip onto the stencil at this point, the slip (or underglaze) would ooze out into that air space, ruining my tile design. I'd have to start all over. So, take your time gently rolling your stencil down onto the clay.

You don't want to use great force to mash the stencil down into the clay, because then the mylar *would* stick, corn starch or no. But you do want to be sure that no part of the stencil has an air bubble 'floating' between the stencil and the clay surface.

After rolling, you can use the tip of your finger to gently press down any little bits of the design that seem to keep stubbornly popping up.

Here, I'm brushing my white slip onto the Knight Templar stencil...

And, my brown underglaze onto the fleur-de-lis stencil.

 You can't leave that slip and/or underglaze sitting there long enough for it to dry a bit and become easier to handle. Because, trust me from years of experience with this process, that mylar WILL begin sticking to your clay before very much longer. So, wait maybe 5 minutes, no more than 10, and slowly lift your stencil off the clay. You can use your needle tool to carefully prick up a corner of the stencil, to get you started. I don't show it in this photo, but for large stencils like this one (the Knight is 10" long), it's a good idea to lift about half the stencil, as you see in the photo, then use your other hand to begin lifting from the other end of the stencil at the same time.

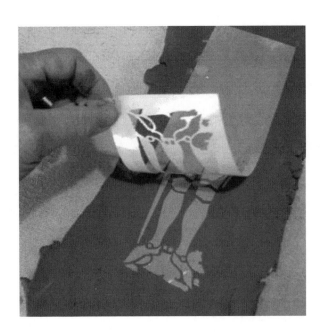

As you see from the above photo, I haven't yet cut the shape of the tile. When you used your rolling pin to adhere the stencil to the clay, the outline of the stencil will leave a faint line in the clay, and you can use that as your guide to cut the shape of the tile with your pizza cutter.

Or, as I'm doing here with the fleur-de-lis tile, you can cut your tile shape even before lifting off your stencil. Either way works just fine.

And, voila! Here we are—two brand new, gorgeous tiles, ready for drying and firing!

Once you've mastered this process, you can turn out a great many tiles in a single afternoon's work. Let's say you wanted 10 of these fleur-de-lis tiles for your backsplash. Roll out a large slab of clay to the desired thickness, make your first tile as we just did, then rinse off your stencil and start right in on the next tile. Remember though, that your stencil must be perfectly dry before you press it into the clay. When I'm doing this 'assembly line work,' I'll lay out a thick bath towel on the counter, lay the rinsed, wet stencil on it, and fold the towel over the stencil. Pat it, but don't rub back and forth or you risk tearing the little incised lines in your stencil. Then, when the stencil feels dry, brush it with corn starch, just to be sure.

And now, a last note about stencils—they're reversible! Some designs look quite pretty as a matched set of tiles, particularly with opposite facing designs like the Stained Glass Angel.

VARIATIONS AND AFTER-THOUGHTS

While working on this book, I received a commission for some custom tiles from a lady in California. She loves the images of crowns and wants to incorporate such images into her tile backsplash. She asked for the base tiles to be finished in a pale dove gray, with the design done in silver. So, while working on that commission, I'm able to show you yet another interesting way to use stencils with tile—that is, use them as templates for drawing out your designs on a commercial bisque tile. I have a set of chess-piece stencils from The Stencil Library, among which are two images of crowns, the king's and the queen's, so I'm using them as my templates.

I've painted my tiles with several coats of pale gray underglaze, and let it dry for several hours. Then, I set the stencil on the tile and traced the design, using a pencil with a blunt, rounded tip. You don't want to use a sharp pencil, because your object here isn't to cut into the underglaze, but to draw on it.

I am painting in the crowns with a small artist's brush, using Duncan's Antique Pewter Glaze.

I'll fire the tiles to the recommended temperature for that glaze. Then, I'll cover the tiles with a clear gloss glaze, wiping it away from the crown designs. Then, I'll glaze fire the tiles again.

Another interesting variation uses both your stamps and your stencils. Use a 'frame' stamp such as the Egyptian frame in this photo to impress a new tile.

(The stamp is at the top of the photo—the tile is at the bottom.) Bisque fire the tile and then use a small Egyptian-themed stencil to draw and paint a design on the tile.

In Conclusion

Thanks for reading my book—I hope it was helpful to you! If you'd like to see some of the many tiles and molds I've made using the methods described here, you can find me at Etsy.com.

www.joliefairemedieval.etsy.com

And watch for my other 'Creating Custom Art Tiles' books!

Creating Custom Art Tiles: The Moravian Method

Creating Custom Art Tiles: Slips and Presses

Creating Custom Art Tiles: Encaustics and Etchings

Creating Custom Art Tiles: Medieval Tiles

Printed in Great Britain
by Amazon.co.uk, Ltd.,
Marston Gate.